# Connect

## SECOND EDITION

# Jack C. Richards
# Carlos Barbisan
### with Chuck Sandy
### and Lisa A. Hutchins

# Workbook **3**

## CAMBRIDGE
UNIVERSITY PRESS

# CAMBRIDGE
## UNIVERSITY PRESS

University Printing House, Cambridge CB2 8BS, United Kingdom

One Liberty Plaza, 20th Floor, New York, NY 10006, USA

477 Williamstown Road, Port Melbourne, VIC 3207, Australia

314–321, 3rd Floor, Plot 3, Splendor Forum, Jasola District Centre, New Delhi – 110025, India

103 Penang Road, #05-06/07, Visioncrest Commercial, Singapore 238467

Cambridge University Press is part of the University of Cambridge.

It furthers the University's mission by disseminating knowledge in the pursuit of education, learning and research at the highest international levels of excellence.

www.cambridge.org
Information on this title: www.cambridge.org/9780521737166

First published 2004
Second edition 2009

40  39  38

Printed in Poland by Opolgraf

*A catalog record for this publication is available from the British Library*

ISBN  978-0-521-73712-8  Student's Book 3 (English)
ISBN  978-0-521-73713-5  Student's Book 3 (Portuguese)
ISBN  978-0-521-73716-6  Workbook 3 (English)
ISBN  978-0-521-73717-3  Workbook 3 (Portuguese)
ISBN  978-0-521-73718-0  Teacher's Edition 3 (English)
ISBN  978-0-521-73719-7  Teacher's Edition 3 (Portuguese)
ISBN  978-0-521-73715-9  Class Audio CDs

*Art direction, photo research, and layout services:* A+ comunicação
*Book design:* Adventure House, NYC

# Table of Contents

# New friends

**1** Complete the questions with *Do* or *Does* and the verbs in the box. Then answer the questions.

☐ get up   ☐ have   ☑ like   ☐ listen   ☐ play   ☐ stay up

1. **Q:** _Do_ they _like_ cake?          **A:** (yes) _Yes, they do._
2. **Q:** _____ you _____ tennis?          **A:** (no) _____
3. **Q:** _____ he _____ early?          **A:** (yes) _____
4. **Q:** _____ you _____ to salsa music?          **A:** (no) _____
5. **Q:** _____ she _____ any sisters?          **A:** (no) _____
6. **Q:** _____ she _____ late?          **A:** (yes) _____

**2** Look at the information. Then write questions and complete the answers with *Ana* or *Ben*.

Name: Ana Suarez          Age: 13

Brothers and sisters: two sisters

Things I like / don't like: I play basketball.
I like ice cream. I listen to rock music.
I get up at 6:30 in the morning, but I don't like to
get up early.

Something interesting about me: I have a
cat. His name is Gatto.

Name: Ben Harding          Age: 14

Brothers and sisters: one brother, one sister

Things I like / don't like: I like pizza. I like
rap music. I play soccer. I don't like to go
shopping. It's boring.


Something interesting about me: I have a
new computer! I have my own Web site.

1. **Q:** (who) _Who has a cat?_
   **A:** _____ does. Her cat's name is Gatto.

2. **Q:** (how many) _____
   **A:** _____ has one brother.

3. **Q:** (what) _____
   **A:** _____ plays soccer.

4. **Q:** (how many) _____
   **A:** _____ has two sisters.

5. **Q:** (how) _____
   **A:** _____ is 14.

6. **Q:** (what) _____
   **A:** _____ gets up at 6:30.

7. **Q:** (what) _____
   **A:** _____ likes pizza.

8. **Q:** (who) _____
   **A:** _____ does. It's a fun Web site.

**1** **Complete the conversation with the sentences in the box.**

☐ Is she making chicken and rice?

☐ Mom makes delicious hamburgers!

☐ No, she isn't.

☐ She's cooking dinner.

☑ What's she doing?

☐ What's she making?

**Wayne** Hi, Joseline. Where's Mom?

**Joseline** She's in the kitchen.

**Wayne** Hmm. _What's she doing?_ _____

**Joseline** _____

**Wayne** Cool! _____

**Joseline** _____

**Wayne** Oh, too bad. Chicken and rice is my favorite. _____

**Joseline** Hamburgers and french fries.

**Wayne** Great! _____

**2** **Complete the sentences with the correct forms of the verbs in the box.**

☐ eat   ☐ feed   ☑ have   ☐ play   ☐ read   ☐ sleep   ☐ walk   ☐ watch

I'm not at school today. It's Saturday. So, I
_have_ a lot of time to play. On Saturdays,
I usually _____ magazines and _____
TV, but today is different. I have a new
dog. His name is Max. Today, I'm going to
_____ him in the park. He loves to go
outside and _____ ball. Right now, I'm
_____ Max some dog food. He's really
cute. He _____ next to my bed at night.
Oh, no! Max doesn't like his dog food, so
he's _____ my mother's shoe!

# Mini-review

**1** **Look at the pictures. Then write questions and answers.**

1. **Q:** What sport does Paul play?

   **A:** *He plays basketball.*

   **Q:** Is he playing now?

   **A:** *Yes, he is.*

2. **Q:** _____

   **A:** Shelly gets up at 5:45 a.m.

   **Q:** _____

   **A:** Yes, she goes to school early.

3. **Q:** _____

   **A:** Bradley has three dogs.

   **Q:** _____

   **A:** No, he isn't feeding the dogs now.

4. **Q:** Who likes to skateboard?

   **A:** _____

   **Q:** Do they have skateboards?

   **A:** _____

**2** **Look at the picture of Nelly. Then write present continuous questions and short answers about her.**

1. **Q:** *Is Nelly watching TV?*

   **A:** *No, she isn't.*

2. **Q:** _____

   **A:** _____

3. **Q:** _____

   **A:** _____

4. **Q:** _____

   **A:** _____

# My new school

**1** Write sentences with *have to* or *don't have to*. Use your own information.

1. (wear a uniform) *I don't have to wear a uniform.*

2. (clean my room) _____

3. (walk to school) _____

4. _____

5. _____

**2** Look at Leila's to-do list. She has checked the things she has to do every day. Write questions and answers about Leila's day. Use the correct forms of *have to* or *don't have to*.

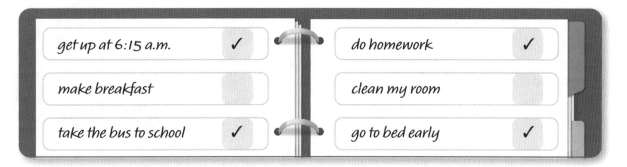

| get up at 6:15 a.m. ✓ | do homework ✓ |
| make breakfast | clean my room |
| take the bus to school ✓ | go to bed early ✓ |

1. **Q:** *Does she have to get up at 6:15 a.m.?*
   **A:** *Yes, she does.* OR *Yes. She has to get up at 6:15 a.m.*

2. **Q:** _____
   **A:** _____

3. **Q:** _____
   **A:** _____

4. **Q:** _____
   **A:** _____

5. **Q:** _____
   **A:** _____

6. **Q:** _____
   **A:** _____

**3** Write questions and answers with *have to* or *don't have to*.

1. **Q:** (students / take gym class) *Do students have to take gym class?*
   **A:** (yes) *Yes, they do.* OR *Yes. They have to take gym class.*

2. **Q:** (teachers / buy lunch in the cafeteria) _____
   **A:** (no) _____

3. **Q:** (you / wear a uniform) _____
   **A:** (yes) _____

4. **Q:** (soccer players / practice every day) _____
   **A:** (no) _____

**1  Answer the questions with your own information.**

1. Would you like to eat ice cream now? _Yes, I would._ OR _No, I wouldn't._
2. Would you like to make a Web site? _____
3. Would you like to make dinner tonight? _____
4. Would you like to get some exercise today? _____
5. Would you like to meet some new people? _____
6. Would you like to do your homework this afternoon? _____

**2  Look at the pictures of after-school activities. Then write questions.**

1. **A** _Would you like to join the volleyball club?_

   **B** Yes, I would.

2. **A** _____

   **B** Yes, I would.

3. **A** _____

   **B** No, I wouldn't.

4. **A** _____

   **B** No, I wouldn't.

5. **A** _____

   **B** Yes, I would.

6. **A** _____

   **B** Yes, I would.

**1** **Read the e-mail quickly. What class is really hard?**

_____

To: mrty@gc.com
From: trrnce@gc.com
Subject: College and Boston

## I don't have to get up early.

Hello, Marty!

How are you? I'm fine, but I miss you. It's my second week here at college. I was nervous at first – I didn't know anyone. But I'm overcoming my fear and I'm starting to like it.

I don't have to get up early because all my classes start late. I have to do a lot of homework every day. My ecology class is really hard, but I like it.

Boston is an exciting city. The food is good. I'm eating oysters right now at a cool little restaurant. Last weekend I learned how to row a boat and navigate it down a river. I'd like to join the boating club.

How is high school? Do you have to go to soccer practice every Saturday?

Say hi to Mom and Dad.

Your brother,

Terrance

**2** **Circle the correct words to complete the sentences.**

1. (Oysters / Fear) come from the ocean. I love to eat them.

2. My sister wants to study (college / ecology).

3. It's not easy to (get up / overcome my fear) of the water.

4. I'd like to (start / row) a boat down a river.

**3** **Read the e-mail in Part 1 slowly. Answer the questions.**

1. Is Terrance overcoming his fear? _Yes, he is._____

2. Does Terrance have to get up early every day? _____

3. How much homework does he have to do every day? _____

4. Does he like Boston? _____

5. What's Terrance doing right now? _____

6. Would he like to join the boating club? _____

**1**   **Number the sentences in the correct order.**

_____ No, I don't. Why?

_____ Yes, I would. What movie do you want to see?

__1__ Do you have to do your homework now?

_____ That sounds good to me!

_____ I'd like to see *Super Dog*.

_____ Would you like to go to the movies with me?

**2**   **Write questions in the present continuous. Then answer the questions.**

1. **Q:** (Shelley / play soccer) *Is Shelley playing soccer?* _____

   **A:** (no) *No, she isn't.* _____

2. **Q:** (what / Ivan / do) _____

   **A:** (listen to music) _____

3. **Q:** (you / do homework) _____

   **A:** (yes) _____

4. **Q:** (what / Luciana / eat) _____

   **A:** (pizza) _____

5. **Q:** (what / Lucas / read) _____

   **A:** (a magazine) _____

6. **Q:** (Walter / buy comic books) _____

   **A:** (no) _____

**3**   **Complete the conversations with the sentences in the box.**

> ☐ Celia does.
> ☐ Does Francisco have to do homework tonight?
> ☑ He has three sisters.
> ☐ Is Mr. da Silva talking on the phone?
> ☐ No, they don't.
> ☐ She's watching her favorite TV show.
> ☐ What time does Abbie get up?
> ☐ Would you like to eat dinner now?

1. **A** How many sisters does Shawn have?

   **B** *He has three sisters.* _____

2. **A** What's Stella doing?

   **B** _____

3. **A** _____

   **B** No, he doesn't.

4. **A** _____

   **B** Yes, I would.

5. **A** _____

   **B** She gets up at 6:30 a.m.

6. **A** _____

   **B** Yes, he is.

7. **A** Who likes pop music?

   **B** _____

8. **A** Do students have to eat lunch in the cafeteria?

   **B** _____

**1** **Write the verbs in the simple past.**

1. skate _____skated_____
2. ask _____
3. visit _____
4. try _____
5. rent _____

6. enjoy _____
7. listen _____
8. study _____
9. arrive _____
10. dance _____

**2** **Rewrite the sentences in the simple past.**

1. We play basketball in the park.
   _We played basketball in the park._

2. Leo cleans his room after school.
   _____

3. The students walk to school.
   _____

4. We shop at the mall on Oak Street.
   _____

5. Kathy calls her friends from the beach.
   _____

6. I stay at home on Monday night.
   _____

7. They race home after school.
   _____

8. You want to go to Venezuela.
   _____

9. She practices the piano.
   _____

10. He needs new sneakers.
   _____

**3** **Write sentences in the simple past about what you did last week.**

1. _I rented some DVDs._
2. _____
3. _____
4. _____

5. _____
6. _____
7. _____
8. _____

# Our trip to Peru

**1** **Match the verbs to the correct simple past forms.**

| | | | |
|---|---|---|---|
| 1. answer _o_ | 10. make ____ | a. gave | j. saw |
| 2. buy ____ | 11. meet ____ | b. made | k. bought |
| 3. drink ____ | 12. see ____ | c. ate | l. got |
| 4. eat ____ | 13. sleep ____ | d. took | m. slept |
| 5. fly ____ | 14. snorkel ____ | e. wrote | n. went |
| 6. get ____ | 15. stop ____ | f. had | o. answered |
| 7. give ____ | 16. take ____ | g. snorkeled | p. watched |
| 8. go ____ | 17. watch ____ | h. drank | q. flew |
| 9. have ____ | 18. write ____ | i. stopped | r. met |

**2** **Choose the correct forms of the verbs to complete the sentences.**

1. I love my new camera. I ((take)/ took) pictures all the time.
2. Carlita (meet / met) some cool people at the school dance last week.
3. Mr. Stevens travels a lot. He (flies / flew) to a different place every month.
4. They (buy / bought) a new house last summer.
5. We went to the museum. We (see / saw) a lot of beautiful paintings.
6. There's no juice in the refrigerator. I (drink / drank) it yesterday.

**3** **Complete the text about Laurie's trip to Mexico with the simple past.**

My name's Laurie. I ___went___ (go) to Mexico with my family last summer. We _____ (fly) to Cancún and _____ (stay) in a hotel near the beach. We _____ (eat) at different restaurants every day. We _____ (try) different kinds of food. I _____ (like) the chicken mole. One day, we _____ (visit) the ruins at Chichén Itzá. The ruins are really beautiful, so I _____ (take) a lot of pictures to show my friends. My sister Tori _____ (buy) some pretty jewelry. In Cozumel, a guide _____ (give) us a tour of the island. My brother _____ (get) some cool T-shirts. We _____ (meet) a lot of nice people, and we _____ (have) a great time on our vacation.

# Mini-review

**1** Complete the chart with the simple past forms of the verbs in the box.

☑ arrive ☐ fly ☐ listen ☐ see ☐ try
☐ dance ☐ give ☐ meet ☐ shop ☐ visit
☑ drink ☐ go ☐ plan ☐ sleep ☐ walk
☐ eat ☐ learn ☐ rent ☐ take ☐ write

| Regular | | Irregular | |
|---|---|---|---|
| _arrived_ | _____ | _drank_ | _____ |
| _____ | _____ | _____ | _____ |
| _____ | _____ | _____ | _____ |
| _____ | _____ | _____ | _____ |

**2** Complete the sentences with the simple past forms of the verbs in the box.

☑ learn ☐ practice ☐ stay ☐ visit
☐ play ☐ race ☐ try ☐ watch

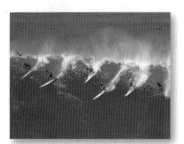

1. Jerome _____learned_____ how to surf.

2. Alicia and her sister _____ a soccer game on TV.

3. Simone _____ at a beautiful hotel.

4. Hal _____ a museum on his vacation.

5. Tomiko _____ a lot of new foods.

6. Juan and Rosario _____ English.

7. Lucy _____ volleyball on the beach.

8. Mr. Parker _____ a dune buggy down the beach.

**3** What did Candace do on her vacation? Write sentences.

1. (fly to Florida) _She flew to Florida._____

2. (eat in many restaurants) _____

3. (go to the beach) _____

4. (buy souvenirs) _____

5. (meet new people) _____

6. (take pictures) _____

7. (write postcards) _____

8. (sleep late every day) _____

# Lesson 7 · School festival

**1** Look at the pictures. Then write questions and complete the answers.

1. **A** _Did you win a prize?_

   **B** _Yes, I did._ I won a stuffed animal.

2. **A** _____

   **B** _____ I went on a lot of rides.

3. **A** _____

   **B** _____ I don't like fun houses!

4. **A** _____

   **B** _____ I don't like to dance.

5. **A** _____

   **B** _____ I played some fun games.

6. **A** _____

   **B** _____ I don't like cotton candy.

**2** Write questions and answers. Then match the questions to the answers.

1. exercise

   **Q:** _Did you exercise?_ _f_

2. study English

   **Q:** _____ ___

3. buy any raffle tickets

   **Q:** _____ ___

4. join the chess club

   **Q:** _____ ___

5. win any prizes

   **Q:** _____ ___

6. eat cotton candy

   **Q:** _____ ___

a. yes / buy five raffle tickets

   **A:** _____

b. yes / win a stuffed animal

   **A:** _____

c. no / join the drama club

   **A:** _____

d. no / eat ice cream

   **A:** _____

e. no / study science

   **A:** _____

f. yes / run

   **A:** _Yes, I did. I ran._ OR _Yes. I ran._

# Weekend fun

**1 Write negative simple past sentences.**

1. Danielle / go to a concert
   _Danielle didn't go to a concert._

2. they / see a movie
   _____

3. Calvin / have fun on Friday
   _____

4. I / buy a new magazine
   _____

5. we / talk on the phone
   _____

6. Tony / go to a party
   _____

7. Cecilia / do a lot of homework
   _____

8. the students / go to the school festival
   _____

**2 Look at Harvey's responses to a survey about weekend activities.
Then write sentences about what he did and didn't do.**

Check (✓) the things you did last weekend.

☐ play video games      ☐ talk on the phone

☑ read magazines      ☑ listen to music

☐ go to the park      ☑ go to a party

☐ do homework      ☐ eat at a restaurant

☑ go downtown      ☑ sleep late

1. _He didn't play video games._
2. _____
3. _____
4. _____
5. _____

6. _____
7. _____
8. _____
9. _____
10. _____

**3 What did you do last weekend? Write four sentences about the things
you did and four sentences about the things you didn't do.**

1. _____
2. _____
3. _____
4. _____
5. _____
6. _____
7. _____
8. _____

**1** Read the Web site quickly. Check (✓) the animals the Web site talks about.

- ☐ fish
- ☐ frogs
- ☐ horse
- ☐ iguana
- ☐ parrot
- ☐ sea lions
- ☐ tortoise
- ☐ whale

www.animalsightings.gc

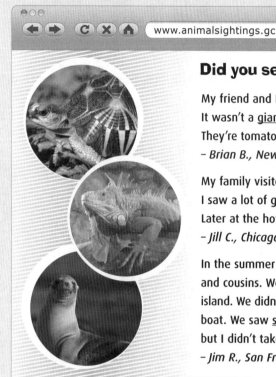

### Did you see any animals this summer? Tell us.

My friend and I saw a radiated tortoise at the Bronx Zoo yesterday. It wasn't a <u>giant</u> tortoise, but it was big. I also saw a lot of little red frogs. They're tomato frogs, and they're <u>endangered</u>. They're really beautiful.
– *Brian B., New York*

My family visited Mexico this summer. We went on a tour of the desert. I saw a lot of great <u>scenery</u> in the desert, but I didn't see any animals. Later at the hotel I saw an iguana in a tree in the garden. I was happy.
– *Jill C., Chicago*

In the summer I <u>went</u> to Raspberry Island in Alaska with my aunt, uncle, and cousins. We had a great time. We went on a boat tour around the island. We didn't <u>snorkel</u> – it was too cold. But we saw a lot of fish from the boat. We saw <u>sea lions</u> and a whale, too. I took pictures of the sea lions, but I didn't take any pictures of the whales. They were too far away.
– *Jim R., San Francisco*

**2** Complete the conversation with the underlined words from Part 1.

**Tom** Where did you go this summer, Jane?

**Jane** I __went__ to San Diego!

**Tom** Did you _____ in the ocean?

**Jane** Yes, I did. I saw a _____ fish. It was really big!

**Tom** Cool! Did you see any _____ animals on your trip?

**Jane** No, I didn't. But I saw some _____ . They're really cute.

**Tom** Did you enjoy the _____ there?

**Jane** Yes. The water and the flowers were so beautiful there.

**3** Read the Web site in Part 1 slowly. Who did these things? Write *Brian*, *Jill*, or *Jim*.

1. Visited a zoo: *Brian*
2. Saw an endangered animal: _____
3. Went to an island: _____
4. Took a picture: _____
5. Traveled with family: _____ and _____
6. Went on a tour: _____ and _____

# Check Yourself

**1** **Match the questions to the answers.**

1. Did Melvin go to a concert last night? _e_
2. Did you do your English homework? ____
3. Did Susanna eat lunch at 12:00? ____
4. Did Gina have a good time at the party? ____
5. Did Ann and Sid watch the fireworks? ____
6. Did Mr. Valdez buy a new camera? ____

a. Yes, she did. She had a great time at the party.
b. No. She ate lunch at 1:00.
c. No. He bought a new CD player.
d. Yes, I did. I finished my report for English.
e. No, he didn't. He went to a movie.
f. Yes. They watched them on TV.

**2** **Complete the sentences about Leah's vacation with the simple past.**

1. (go to London) I _went to London_____ .
2. (fly there) My family and I _____ .
3. (take seven hours) It _____ .
4. (visit Buckingham Palace) We _____ .
5. (buy souvenirs) My sister _____ .
6. (take great pictures) My father _____ .
7. (meet some new people) I _____ .
8. (eat good food) We _____ .

**3** **Steve and Flora went to a party last night. Look at the chart.**
**Then write sentences about what they did and didn't do.**

|       | eat pizza | dance | play games | go home early |
|-------|-----------|-------|------------|---------------|
| Steve | ✗         | ✗     | ✓          | ✗             |
| Flora | ✓         | ✓     | ✗          | ✓             |

Steve

1. _Steve didn't eat pizza._____
2. _____
3. _____
4. _____

Flora

5. _____
6. _____
7. _____
8. _____

# A homestay

**1 Choose the correct words to complete the sentences.**

1. Ellen spent the day at the beach. She was ___relaxed___ (relaxed / frustrated).

2. Kurt spilled his drink on the table. He was _____ (glad / embarrassed).

3. Ann and Al didn't pass the English test. They were _____ (frustrated / glad).

4. Ken got tickets to see his favorite rock band. He was _____ (excited / frustrated).

5. Christina didn't like flying. She was _____ (relaxed / worried).

6. We walked for eight hours. We were _____ (exhausted / embarrassed).

**2 Complete Mike's e-mail message about his homestay with *was, were, wasn't,* or *weren't.***

To: Sam

Hi, Sam!

Well, Kevin and I made it. We flew all the way to Germany to begin our homestay. The trip was very long. Kevin ___was___ exhausted, but I _____ . I _____ happy! We met our host family, Mr. and Mrs. Schmidt, at the airport. We _____ excited. They spoke English really well. We _____ surprised! I don't speak German well, but Kevin does. I _____ worried, but Kevin _____ . Mr. and Mrs. Schmidt made us a great dinner. Kevin didn't like the German food. He _____ embarrassed. Mr. and Mrs. Schmidt just laughed. They _____ surprised at all. Mrs. Schmidt made Kevin some pasta. Kevin and I _____ a little homesick last night, but we're OK now. Mr. and Mrs. Schmidt are great, so we're glad to be here.
– Mike

**3 Write sentences with *was* or *were*.**

1. Eve / homesick
   _Eve was homesick._

2. Carlo and Maria / not worried
   _____

3. Scott / glad
   _____

4. Jeremy and Max / exhausted
   _____

5. Rebecca / relaxed
   _____

6. Mr. Hill / not embarrassed
   _____

7. you / not surprised
   _____

8. Yuko / not frustrated
   _____

# Getting away

**1 Look at the pictures. Then answer the questions.**

1. **Q:** Were they at a
   dude ranch?

   **A:** *Yes, they were.*

2. **Q:** Were they at a
   dance club?

   **A:** _____

3. **Q:** Was Al at a
   ski resort?

   **A:** _____

4. **Q:** Were you on a safari?

   **A:** _____

5. **Q:** Was it chilly?

   **A:** _____

6. **Q:** Was it a big hotel?

   **A:** _____

**2 Write questions and answers.**

1. **Q:** (Sasha / at a ski resort) *Was Sasha at a ski resort?* _____
   **A:** (yes) *Yes, she was.* _____

2. **Q:** (Mr. and Mrs. Miller / in Brazil) _____
   **A:** (no) _____

3. **Q:** (the weather / nice) _____
   **A:** (no) _____

4. **Q:** (you / at a theme park) _____
   **A:** (yes) _____

5. **Q:** (your cousins / at a dude ranch) _____
   **A:** (no) _____

6. **Q:** (the hotel / new) _____
   **A:** (yes) _____

7. **Q:** (Annie / at home) _____
   **A:** (no) _____

# Mini-review

**1 Complete the sentences with *was*, *were*, *wasn't*, or *weren't*.**

1. Brad fell out of the raft. He ___was___ embarrassed.
2. Adam _____ homesick. He missed his family.
3. Emilio and Juan slept a lot on Monday. They _____ exhausted on Tuesday.
4. Ted _____ nervous on the airplane. He was very relaxed.
5. Mr. and Mrs. Gray couldn't read the Japanese tour book. They _____ frustrated.
6. Sook Jin got an A on her English test. She _____ glad.

**2 Complete the conversation with the sentences in the box.**

| |
|---|
| ☐ No, it wasn't.      ☑ Were you on vacation last week? |
| ☐ Was it cold?      ☐ Yes, it was. |
| ☐ Was the weather good?      ☐ Yes, I was. |
| ☐ Were you and your family on vacation last week?      ☐ Yes, we were. |

**Tom** Hi, Anna. *Were you on vacation last week?*

**Anna** _____ I was at a ski resort in Colorado.

**Tom** Wow! _____

**Anna** _____ It was very cold, and it snowed every day.

**Tom** That's great.

**Anna** How about you? _____

**Tom** _____ We didn't go on a trip, but we went to the Adventure Land theme park one day.

**Anna** _____

**Tom** _____ It rained. But we had a good time.

**3 Write questions. Then write answers with your own information.**

1. your friends / at the mall yesterday

   **Q:** *Were your friends at the mall yesterday?*      **A:** *Yes, they were.*

2. the weather / nice last month

   **Q:** _____      **A:** _____

3. your English class / interesting yesterday

   **Q:** _____      **A:** _____

4. your classmates / on vacation last week

   **Q:** _____      **A:** _____

5. your best friend / in Puerto Rico last summer

   **Q:** _____      **A:** _____

# Explorers

**1** **Answer the questions.**

1. **Q:** When did you travel to Colombia?
   **A:** (three years ago) _I traveled to Colombia three years ago._

2. **Q:** When did Sheila start her project?
   **A:** (two weeks ago) _____

3. **Q:** What did Ramon write about?
   **A:** (Spanish explorers) _____

4. **Q:** Where did you go last night?
   **A:** (library) _____

5. **Q:** What did they study yesterday?
   **A:** (math) _____

6. **Q:** Where did Mrs. Melfi go last summer?
   **A:** (Venezuela) _____

**2** **Read about Roald Amundsen. Then write questions and answers with information from the article.**

Roald Amundsen was a famous explorer. He and another explorer, Robert Scott, raced each other to the South Pole. Roald Amundsen arrived at the South Pole before Robert Scott. He arrived at the South Pole on December 14, 1911. He used 48 dogs and four sleds. Scott arrived at the South Pole a month later, in January 1912. Scott used horses on his trip to the South Pole.

1. when / Roald Amundsen / arrive at the South Pole
   **Q:** _When did Roald Amundsen arrive at the South Pole?_
   **A:** _He arrived at the South Pole on December 14, 1911._

2. what / Roald Amundsen / use on his trip
   **Q:** _____
   **A:** _____

3. when / Robert Scott / arrive at the South Pole
   **Q:** _____
   **A:** _____

4. what / Robert Scott / use on his trip
   **Q:** _____
   **A:** _____

# Up and away

**1 Look at the information. Then answer the questions about Mae Jemison.**

Mae Jemison, Astronaut
– Born October 17th, 1956, in Decatur, Alabama
– Completed astronaut training in 1988
– Flew into space for the first time in 1992
– Name of shuttle was *Endeavour*
– Left NASA in 1993

1. When was Mae Jemison born? *She was born on October 17th, 1956.*

2. Where was Mae Jemison born? _____

3. What did Mae Jemison do in 1988? _____

4. When was Mae Jemison's first flight? _____

5. What was the name of the shuttle she flew on? _____

6. When did Mae Jemison leave NASA? _____

**2 Complete the conversations. Use the simple past.**

1. **A** *When was* your first trip?

   **B** *It was* three years ago.

   OR *My first trip was* three years ago.

2. **A** _____ his first train ride?

   **B** _____ 10 years ago.

3. **A** _____ you last night?

   **B** _____ at home.

4. **A** _____ they do last Saturday?

   **B** _____ swimming and shopping.

5. **A** _____ Alison go last year?

   **B** _____ to Mexico.

6. **A** _____ Alan Shepard?

   **B** _____ a famous astronaut.

**3 Look at the underlined information. Then write questions.**

1. **Q:** *Where were you born?*     **A:** I was born in <u>Rio de Janeiro</u>.

2. **Q:** _____     **A:** I <u>did homework</u> and <u>went to the library</u> yesterday.

3. **Q:** _____     **A:** His English test was <u>last week</u>.

4. **Q:** _____     **A:** I visited <u>my aunt and uncle</u>.

5. **Q:** _____     **A:** <u>David and Dee</u> were at the mall.

6. **Q:** _____     **A:** My homestay was in <u>Lisbon, Portugal</u>.

# Get Connected
## UNIT 3

**1 Read the article quickly. Underline the verbs in the simple past.**

## A Modern Hero

Susan Butcher is a modern hero in Alaska. She moved from Boston to Alaska in 1974. She loved dogs and dogsled racing, and she wanted to take part in the Iditarod. The Iditarod is a race with a dog team, and it's about 1,000 miles (1,610 kilometers) long.

Susan learned important skills for the race from local people. She raced a few times but didn't win until 1986. Susan also won the race in 1987, 1988, and 1990. Susan was the second woman to win the race. The first woman to win was Libby Riddles. She won the race in 1985.

In 2005, Susan got very sick, and she died in 2006. Today, the first Sunday in March in Alaska is "Susan Butcher Day."

**2 Circle the word that is different.**

1. journey     trip        (skill)
2. glad        happy       frustrated
3. miles       journey     kilometers
4. begins      starts      long

**3 Read the article in Part 1 slowly. Answer the questions.**

1. When did Susan Butcher move to Alaska? _She moved to Alaska in 1974._

2. What animal did she love? _____

3. What did Susan learn from local people? _____

4. How many times did Susan win the Iditarod? _____

5. Was she the first woman winner? _____

6. When did she die? _____

**1 Check (✓) the correct responses.**

1. Were Omar and Marisol at the party?
   - ☑ No, they weren't.
   - ☐ Yes, she was.

2. When did Wally buy the book?
   - ☐ He's buying it now.
   - ☐ He bought it last week.

3. What did Elizabeth do yesterday?
   - ☐ She made a chocolate cake.
   - ☐ She's going to school.

4. Where was Janine last week?
   - ☐ She was in California.
   - ☐ She's in California.

5. Was the weather bad?
   - ☐ No, I wasn't.
   - ☐ No, it wasn't.

6. Were you homesick, Anita?
   - ☐ Yes, I was.
   - ☐ Yes, we were.

7. Where did Mia find the information?
   - ☐ She found it yesterday.
   - ☐ She found it on the Internet.

8. When was John's first day of school?
   - ☐ It was Monday.
   - ☐ Next week.

**2 Complete the conversations with *was*, *wasn't*, *were*, or *weren't*.**

1. **Q:** _Was_ it snowing yesterday?
   **A:** Yes, it _was_ .

2. **Q:** _____ they at Diana's party?
   **A:** Yes, they _____ .

3. **Q:** _____ Oliver and Sam at the mall?
   **A:** No, they _____ .

4. **Q:** _____ Martin at a dude ranch?
   **A:** No, he _____ .

5. **Q:** _____ it a fun party?
   **A:** Yes, it _____ !

6. **Q:** _____ you embarrassed?
   **A:** No, I _____ .

**3 Look at the chart. How did Ms. Tyra's students feel about yesterday's test? Write sentences with *was*, *wasn't*, *were*, or *weren't*.**

|            | Megan | Enzo | Shawn and Elliot |
|------------|:-----:|:----:|:----------------:|
| worried    |   ✗   |  ✓   |        ✓         |
| relaxed    |   ✓   |  ✗   |        ✗         |
| frustrated |   ✗   |  ✓   |        ✓         |

1. _Megan wasn't worried._
2. _____
3. _____
4. _____
5. _____
6. _____
7. _____
8. _____
9. _____

**1** **Complete the sentences with comparative adjectives.**

1. India is ___hotter___ (hot) than Antarctica.

2. A dog can run _____ (fast) than a tortoise.

3. Katie Holmes is _____ (tall) than Tom Cruise.

4. Rio de Janiero is _____ (warm) than Anchorage, Alaska.

5. Brazil is _____ (large) than Peru.

6. An elephant is _____ (heavy) than a giraffe.

7. Iceland is _____ (cold) than Kenya.

8. The Amazon River is _____ (long) than the Ganges River in India.

9. Mount Everest is _____ (high) than Mount Kilimanjaro.

10. The moon is _____ (small) than the sun.

**2** **Write sentences.**

1. cute: cats / rabbits
   _Rabbits are cuter than cats._

2. cold: Costa Rica / Canada
   _____

3. heavy: elephants / birds
   _____

4. slow: airplanes / cars
   _____

5. big: a basketball / a baseball
   _____

6. short: a mouse / a horse
   _____

7. light: a book / a pencil
   _____

8. warm: the sun / the moon
   _____

**3** **Write sentences with your own information.**

1. (tall) _I'm taller than my best friend._

2. (easy) _____

3. (long) _____

4. (friendly) _____

5. (big) _____

6. (busy) _____

**1** **Look at Maria's responses to the survey. Then write sentences about her opinions.**

E-Teen Scene

**Opinion Survey**

More popular ☑ rock music ☐ classical music
More entertaining ☐ movies ☑ concerts
More exciting ☑ basketball ☐ soccer
More delicious ☐ cake ☑ cookies
More difficult ☐ math ☑ English
More useful ☑ computers ☐ cell phones
More challenging ☐ surfing ☑ skateboarding
More interesting ☑ books ☐ TV

1. *Rock music is more popular*
   *than classical music.*
2. _____
3. _____
4. _____

5. _____
6. _____
7. _____
8. _____

**2** **What do you think? Write your opinions. Use comparisons with _more . . . than_.**

1. entertaining: horror movies / action movies
   *I think action movies are more entertaining than horror movies.*

2. relaxing: a beach / a theme park
   _____

3. dangerous: white-water rafting / skiing
   _____

4. delicious: ice cream / chocolate cake
   _____

5. important: math / science
   _____

6. popular: baseball / basketball
   _____

7. useful: the Internet / books
   _____

8. challenging: speaking English / reading English
   _____

ADVENTURE
MOUNTAIN

**1** Look at the chart. Are the statements about these athletes true or false?
Write *T* (true) or *F* (false). Then correct the false statements.

| | **LeBron James** | **Rafael Nadal** | **David Wright** |
|---|---|---|---|
| Born | December 30, 1984 | June 3, 1986 | December 20, 1982 |
| Height | 6 feet, 8 inches (2.03 meters) | 6 feet, 1 inch (1.85 meters) | 6 feet, 1 inch (1.85 meters) |
| Weight | 250 pounds (113.39 kilograms) | 188 pounds (85.27 kilograms) | 208 pounds (94.35 kilograms) |

1. LeBron James is lighter than David Wright. *F*
   *LeBron James is heavier than David Wright.*

2. Rafael Nadal is shorter than LeBron James. _____

3. LeBron James is older than David Wright. _____

4. Rafael Nadal is younger than David Wright. _____

5. Rafael Nadal is heavier than LeBron James. _____

6. David Wright is taller than LeBron James. _____

**2** Complete the conversation. Make sentences with the words in the box
and comparative adjectives. Use *more* when necessary.

- ☐ cats / friendly / dogs
- ☐ I think dogs / friendly / cats
- ☐ I think skiing / safe / white-water rafting
- ☐ I think tennis / hard / soccer
- ☐ pasta / fast to make / pizza
- ☐ pizza / delicious / pasta
- ☑ tennis / difficult / soccer
- ☐ white-water rafting / dangerous / skiing

**Rick** Hi, Allison. What are you doing?

**Allison** I'm taking an opinion survey. Do you agree with this sentence?
*Tennis is more difficult than soccer.*

**Rick** I agree. _____

**Allison** OK, next item. _____

**Rick** I don't know. Cats are OK, but dogs are great.

_____

**Allison** So, you disagree. How about this one? _____

**Rick** White-water rafting and skiing. Hmm. _____
I guess I agree.

**Allison** OK. Last one. _____

**Rick** Wow. I like them both. But it only takes 10 minutes to make pasta.

_____

And that's important when I'm really hungry!

# World trivia

**1** Complete the questions with the superlative forms of the adjectives. Then answer the questions.

1. **Q:** What's _the tallest_ (tall) building in the world?

   **A:** (Burj Dubai) _Burj Dubai is the tallest building in the world._

2. **Q:** What's _____ (large) mall in the U.S.?

   **A:** (the Mall of America) _____

3. **Q:** What's _____ (hot) city in the world?

   **A:** (Bangkok) _____

4. **Q:** What's _____ (long) river in the world?

   **A:** (the Nile) _____

5. **Q:** What's _____ (heavy) snake in the world?

   **A:** (the anaconda) _____

**2** Look at the Web site. Then write simple past questions and answers about dinosaurs. Use superlatives.

1. **Q:** _What was the smartest dinosaur in the world?_

   **A:** _The Troodon was the smartest dinosaur in the world._

2. **Q:** _____

   **A:** _____

3. **Q:** _____

   **A:** _____

4. **Q:** _____

   **A:** _____

5. **Q:** _____

   **A:** _____

# The most

**1** **Complete the article about Ms. Travel-A-Lot's opinions. Use *the most* and the adjectives in the box.**

☐ beautiful ☑ exciting ☐ popular ☐ thrilling
☐ crowded ☐ expensive ☐ relaxing

　　I love to travel. I travel all over the world. Here are some of my favorite places. I think Bangkok is *the most exciting* city in the world. It has fantastic stores, restaurants, and museums. There's always something to do in Bangkok. _____ city in the world is San Francisco. The Golden Gate Bridge and its many parks and gardens make San Francisco a pretty city to visit. I think New York City is _____ city in the United States. In some places, a slice of pizza is five dollars! _____ city in the world is Honolulu. You can sit on Waikiki Beach and enjoy the sun and sand. _____ city in the world is Las Vegas. There are great theme parks to visit, and some hotels even have their own roller coasters! _____ city in the world is Mumbai, India. There are almost 14 million people in Mumbai! And finally, Paris is _____ city in the world. More tourists visit Paris each year than any other city in the world!

**2** **Write questions and answers.**

1. popular city in Brazil / Rio de Janeiro

　**Q:** *What's the most popular city in Brazil?*

　**A:** *Rio de Janeiro is the most popular city in Brazil.*

　　OR *The most popular city in Brazil is Rio de Janeiro.*

2. beautiful city in Canada / Vancouver

　**Q:** _____

　**A:** _____

3. famous statue in New York City / the Statue of Liberty

　**Q:** _____

　**A:** _____

4. exciting city in Japan / Kyoto

　**Q:** _____

　**A:** _____

5. expensive city in the world / Moscow

　**Q:** _____

　**A:** _____

**1** Read the Web site quickly. Match the pictures to the facts in the Web site.

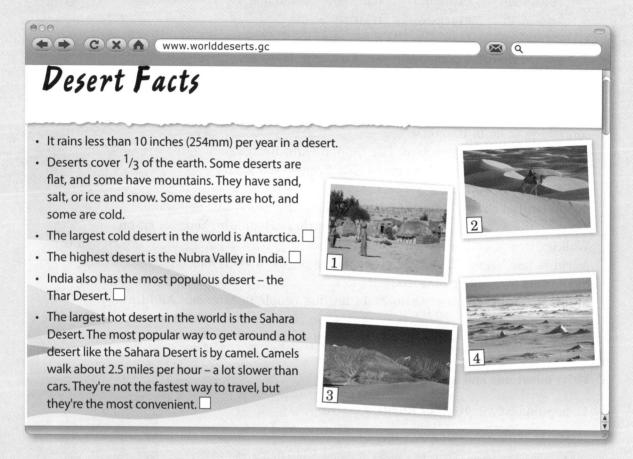

www.worlddeserts.gc

## Desert Facts

- It rains less than 10 inches (254mm) per year in a desert.
- Deserts cover $^1/_3$ of the earth. Some deserts are flat, and some have mountains. They have sand, salt, or ice and snow. Some deserts are hot, and some are cold.
- The largest cold desert in the world is Antarctica. ☐
- The highest desert is the Nubra Valley in India. ☐
- India also has the most populous desert – the Thar Desert. ☐
- The largest hot desert in the world is the Sahara Desert. The most popular way to get around a hot desert like the Sahara Desert is by camel. Camels walk about 2.5 miles per hour – a lot slower than cars. They're not the fastest way to travel, but they're the most convenient. ☐

**2** Circle the correct words to complete the sentences.

1. My mother likes to climb (mountains / deserts).

2. The (heaviest / tallest) building in New York City is the Empire State Building.

3. My sister is the (fastest / highest) driver in the family.

4. The most (popular / populous) snack in the world is potato chips.

**3** Read the Web site in Part 1 slowly. Correct the underlined words in the sentences.

1. Deserts cover ½ of the earth.    *¹/₃*

2. Antarctica is <u>hotter</u> than the Sahara.

3. <u>The Thar Desert</u> is higher than all other deserts.

4. <u>The Nubra Valley</u> is the most populous desert in the world.

5. Camels are the most <u>dangerous</u> way to get around in a desert.

6. Camels are <u>faster</u> than cars.

# Check Yourself

**1** **Number the sentences in the correct order.**

_____ Really? Why do you think he's the most famous actor in the world?

_____ Yes, they are. Now, Sabrina, who's the most beautiful actress in the world?

_____ OK. I agree with you. They're also some of the most thrilling movies around.

_____ Well, I think Tobey Maguire is the most famous actor in the world.

_____ Hmm. I think Penelope Cruz is the most beautiful actress in the world.

_____ He starred in the *Spider–Man* movies. They're some of the most popular movies around.

_1_ Sondra, who's the most famous actor in the world?

**2** **Complete the texts with comparative adjectives. Use _more_ when necessary.**

1. Hi. I'm Monica. I'm 14. I have a sister. Her name is Melissa. She's
   _____*younger*_____ (young) than I am, but she's _____ (tall) than I am.
   My favorite subject is science. I think it's _____ (easy) than English.
   I like pop music, but my sister likes rap. She thinks rap music
   is _____ (popular) than pop. My sister likes movies, but I don't. I think
   concerts are _____ (entertaining) than movies.

2. Hello! I'm Jaime. I just moved to Houston from New York City. Houston is
   _____ (warm) than New York City, but I think New York City is
   _____ (busy) than Houston. My favorite sport is soccer. It's
   _____ (exciting) than baseball! Soccer players run _____ (fast)
   than baseball players. Soccer is _____ (hard) to play, too!

**3** **Write questions and answers about these students in Mrs. Turner's class. Use superlatives.**

**Hank**        **Lorena**        **Brian**        **Jin**

1. **Q:** (fast girl) _Who's the fastest girl in Mrs. Turner's class?_
   **A:** _Jin is the fastest girl in Mrs. Turner's class._

2. **Q:** (strong boy) _____
   **A:** _____

3. **Q:** (smart girl) _____
   **A:** _____

4. **Q:** (tall boy) _____
   **A:** _____

**1** Write the adverbs of manner for the adjectives.

1. comfortable ___*comfortably*___     6. crazy _____

2. regular _____     7. quiet _____

3. careful _____     8. happy _____

4. quick _____     9. important _____

5. slow _____     10. easy _____

**2** Complete the sentences with the correct forms of the adjectives in the box.

☑ careful   ☐ comfortable   ☐ patient   ☐ quick   ☐ quiet   ☐ regular

1. I helped my mom make a cake. She told me to measure
   the flour ___*carefully*___ .

2. Our gym teacher told us to dress _____ today.
   We're learning yoga.

3. Please don't make noise in the library. Study _____ .

4. I go to the gym _____ . I go every day.

5. Dr. Cole will see you in a few minutes. Please wait _____ .

6. Warren can read one book a day. He reads _____ .

**3** Look at the pictures. Then write sentences with adverbs of manner.

☐ careful / crazy     ☐ loud / quiet     ☑ quick / slow     ☐ safe / dangerous

1. (run) ___*Judy runs quickly. Min runs*___
   ___*slowly.*___

2. (sing) _____

3. (ride his bike) _____

4. (dance) _____

# I don't feel well.

**1** **Choose the correct words to complete the sentences.**

1. Where are my eyedrops? My ___allergies___ (sore throat / allergies) are terrible today.

2. I have _____ (a cold / a headache). My head really hurts.

3. I talked too much today. I have _____ (a sore throat / the flu).

4. When I have _____ (the flu / a headache), I eat some chicken soup.

5. I have _____ (allergies / an earache), so my doctor gave me some eardrops.

6. I drink a lot of water when I have _____ (an earache / a cold).

**2** **Write questions and answers.**

1. **Q:** (you / have an earache) _What do you do when you have an earache?_

   **A:** (use warm eardrops) _I use warm eardrops when I have an earache._
   OR _When I have an earache, I use warm eardrops._

2. **Q:** (Julio / have a sore throat) _____

   **A:** (drink hot tea with lemon) _____

3. **Q:** (Linda / have a headache) _____

   **A:** (try to rest in a quiet place) _____

4. **Q:** (Mr. and Mrs. Wells / have colds) _____

   **A:** (drink a lot of water) _____

5. **Q:** (you / have allergies) _____

   **A:** (take some allergy pills) _____

**3** **Complete the conversation.**

**Wendell** I don't feel well. I have a cold, a sore throat, and an earache.

**Mom** Oh, no! That's too bad!

**Wendell** (have a cold) _What do you do when you have a cold?_

**Mom** (take some cold medicine) _____

**Wendell** OK. (a sore throat) _____

**Mom** (drink hot tea with lemon) _____

**Wendell** Yuck! That sounds terrible. (an earache) _____

_____

**Mom** (go to the doctor) _____

**Wendell** The doctor? Oh, no! I don't like to go to the doctor.

**Mom** I know. But you need some eardrops, so I'm calling the doctor right now!

# Mini-review

**1 Complete the weight-training tips with adverbs of manner.**

Health & Fitness

*Weight training is very important. When you lift weights, you make your muscles stronger. Strong muscles can help you run faster and jump higher when you play sports. Read these tips:*

- You can ____easily____ (easy) begin a weight-training program in a gym or a health club.

- Most gyms and health clubs have trainers who can show you how to do each exercise _____ (safe) and _____ (correct).

- Dress _____ (comfortable). Wear sneakers and loose clothing.

- Begin your weight-training program _____ (slow). Start with a few simple exercises.

- Take your time doing each exercise. Don't do the exercises _____ (quick), or you can hurt yourself.

- Go to the gym _____ (regular). It's important to train two to three times a week for the best results.

- Have fun! You're on your way to a strong, healthy body.

**2 Look at the chart. Then write questions and answers.**

|  | **A cold** | **Allergies** |
|---|---|---|
| Melissa | take cold medicine | take allergy pills |
| Manuel and Derek | drink a lot of water | stay inside |
| Natsuko | drink orange juice | use eyedrops |

1. **Q:** *What does Melissa do when she has a cold?*

   **A:** *She takes cold medicine when she has a cold.*

   OR *When she has a cold, she takes cold medicine.*

2. **Q:** _____

   **A:** _____

3. **Q:** _____

   **A:** _____

4. **Q:** _____

   **A:** _____

5. **Q:** _____

   **A:** _____

6. **Q:** _____

   **A:** _____

# Are you healthy?

**1 Complete the sentences with the words in the box.**

> ☐ every day   ☐ once a week   ☐ three times a week   ☐ twice a year
> ☐ every month   ☐ once a year   ☑ twice a day   ☐ never

1. William brushes his teeth _twice a day_ . He brushes them in the morning. Then he brushes them again before he goes to bed.

2. I go to the doctor for a checkup _____ . I usually go once in January and once in July.

3. Kyle feeds his dog, Rex, _____ . He usually feeds Rex in the morning.

4. I celebrate my birthday _____ , on August 29.

5. Liz goes to her violin lesson _____ . It's at 4:00 p.m. every Wednesday.

6. Sara has soccer practice _____ – every Monday, Tuesday, and Thursday.

7. I don't like vegetables at all! I _____ eat them.

8. My parents pay their bills _____ – usually at the end of the month.

**2 Look at Miguel's responses to a survey about health. Then write sentences.**

### Green Street Fitness

| How often do you ... ? | | | |
|---|---|---|---|
| exercise | ☐ every day | ☒ three times a week | ☐ once a week |
| go to the doctor for a checkup | ☒ once a year | ☐ twice a year | ☐ never |
| get a cold or the flu | ☐ once a year | ☒ three times a year | ☐ five or more times a year |
| brush your teeth | ☐ once a day | ☒ twice a day | ☐ three times a day |
| eat fruits and vegetables | ☐ every day | ☐ four or more times a week | ☒ never |
| eat candy and cookies | ☒ every day | ☐ four or more times a week | ☐ never |

1. _He exercises three times a week._
2. _____
3. _____
4. _____
5. _____
6. _____

**3 Write questions. Then answer the questions with your own information.**

1. **Q:** (have a cold) _How often do you have a cold?_   **A:** _I have a cold about three times a year._

2. **Q:** (do yoga) _____   **A:** _____

3. **Q:** (brush your teeth) _____   **A:** _____

4. **Q:** (eat junk food) _____   **A:** _____

5. **Q:** (see the school nurse) _____   **A:** _____

6. **Q:** (go to the dentist) _____   **A:** _____

# Lesson 20 Teen health tips

**1 Complete the sentences with *should* or *shouldn't*.**

1. It's important to eat a healthy breakfast every morning. You _shouldn't_ skip breakfast.

2. You _____ protect your skin. Use sunscreen every day, even in the winter!

3. You _____ sit around and watch TV all day. Be active. Try to exercise for 30 minutes every day.

4. You _____ brush and floss your teeth regularly. It prevents cavities.

5. Eat snacks like fruit, cheese, and vegetables. You _____ eat junk food.

6. You _____ challenge your brain. Read an interesting book or do a crossword puzzle.

**2 Complete the conversations. Write sentences with *should* or *shouldn't* and the verb phrases in the box.**

| | |
|---|---|
| ☑ eat junk food | ☐ stay up late |
| ☐ join the drama club | ☐ take an aspirin |
| ☐ read this new book | ☐ try some chicken soup |
| ☐ skip breakfast | ☐ try yoga |

1. **A** I'm hungry. I want some cookies.

   **B** _You shouldn't eat junk food._ Have an apple.

2. **A** I feel terrible. I have the flu.

   **B** _____

3. **A** I have a headache.

   **B** _____

4. **A** I'm always tired.

   **B** _____

5. **A** I eat breakfast about three times a week.

   **B** Eat breakfast every day. _____

6. **A** I need to relax.

   **B** _____ It's very relaxing.

7. **A** I want to join a club at school.

   **B** _____ It's a lot of fun.

8. **A** I'm bored. I don't know what to do.

   **B** _____ It's really good!

**3 What should you do to be healthy? What shouldn't you do? Write sentences.**

1. _You shouldn't eat junk food._ _____

2. _____

3. _____

4. _____

5. _____

6. _____

**1** **Read the blog quickly. Write the best title in the blog.**

1. A new capoeira fan    2. Studying a martial art is hard.    3. Karate is exciting.

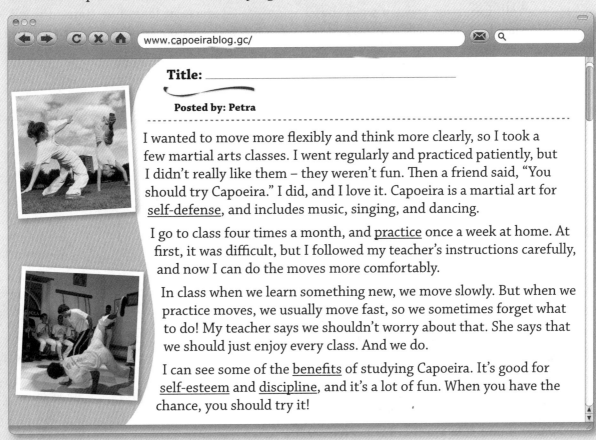

**Title:** _____

**Posted by: Petra**

- - - - - - - - - - - - - - - - - - - - - - - - - - - - - - - - - - - - - - - - - - - - - - -

I wanted to move more flexibly and think more clearly, so I took a few martial arts classes. I went regularly and practiced patiently, but I didn't really like them – they weren't fun. Then a friend said, "You should try Capoeira." I did, and I love it. Capoeira is a martial art for <u>self-defense</u>, and includes music, singing, and dancing.

I go to class four times a month, and <u>practice</u> once a week at home. At first, it was difficult, but I followed my teacher's instructions carefully, and now I can do the moves more comfortably.

In class when we learn something new, we move slowly. But when we practice moves, we usually move fast, so we sometimes forget what to do! My teacher says we shouldn't worry about that. She says that we should just enjoy every class. And we do.

I can see some of the <u>benefits</u> of studying Capoeira. It's good for <u>self-esteem</u> and <u>discipline</u>, and it's a lot of fun. When you have the chance, you should try it!

**2** **Complete the sentences with the underlined words from Part 1.**

1. When you do martial arts regularly, you will see the ___*benefits*___ quickly. You will feel healthier, and your _____ will probably improve, too.

2. You need to _____ a lot to become really good at a martial art.

3. Capoeira is a kind of martial art and teaches _____ skills.

4. To practice something every day you need _____ .

**3** **Read the blog in Part 1 slowly. Circle the correct words to complete the sentences.**

1. Petra didn't like (her martial arts classes / her patient practice / her teacher).

2. A friend told her about (philosophy / Capoeira / self-defense).

3. She practices (four times a week / four times a month / once a week).

4. When they practice moves, they move (quickly / comfortably / slowly).

5. Petra's teacher thinks it's important to (join / study / enjoy every class).

**Your Health    35**

**1 Complete the conversation with *should* or *shouldn't*.**

**Nicole** Hi, Jason. How was your checkup? What did the doctor tell you?

**Jason** My checkup was OK. She gave me a lot of information.

**Nicole** Like what?

**Jason** Well, I exercise twice a week, but I _should_ exercise at least five times a week. Also, I _____ skip breakfast. I _____ eat a big, healthy breakfast every day.

**Nicole** How about sleep?

**Jason** I _____ stay up late. I _____ sleep at least eight hours every night.

**Nicole** What did the doctor say about candy and soda?

**Jason** The doctor said I _____ eat too much candy. She also said that I _____ drink water or milk instead of soda.

**Nicole** That makes sense.

**Jason** And she said I _____ relax a little every day.

**2 Rewrite the sentences with adverbs of manner.**

1. My sister and her friend are quick runners. _They run quickly._

2. Roberta is a slow reader. _____

3. Mrs. Patterson is a careful driver. _____

4. We need to dress in comfortable clothes. _____

5. Raquel is a loud singer. _____

6. Mr. Viera is a patient teacher. _____

7. My friend is a quiet speaker. _____

8. Joanna and Rob are regular exercisers. _____

**3 Complete the conversations with the sentences in the box.**

☐ He studies every day.          ☐ She takes two aspirin.
☐ How often does Hugh exercise?  ☑ What do you do when you're hungry?
☐ I never eat candy.             ☐ What do your friends do when they have the flu?

1. **A** _What do you do when you're hungry?_

   **B** I ask my mother to make me a sandwich.

2. **A** What does Kendra do when she has a headache?

   **B** _____

3. **A** _____

   **B** He exercises a lot! He runs every day.

4. **A** How often do you eat candy?

   **B** _____

5. **A** _____

   **B** They stay in bed and sleep when they have the flu.

6. **A** How often does he study?

   **B** _____

# School fund-raiser

**1** Look at the Roberts family's to-do list. Then write sentences with *be going to*.

**Saturday To-Do List**

do yard work — Mom and Frank
wash windows — Vicky
clean the garage — Dad and Brad
wash the car — Brad
walk dogs — Lisa
do homework — Frank and Brad
make dinner — Mom
babysit — Vicky

1. _Mom and Frank are going to do yard work._
2. _____
3. _____
4. _____
5. _____
6. _____
7. _____
8. _____

**2** Look at the pictures. Then write questions and answers about what these teens are going to do.

1. Lucinda / work at the bake sale

   **Q:** _Is Lucinda going to work at the bake sale?_

   **A:** _Yes, she is._

2. Ken / do yard work

   **Q:** _____

   **A:** _____

3. Hitomi / make dinner

   **Q:** _____

   **A:** _____

4. Chris and Brian / clean the garage

   **Q:** _____

   **A:** _____

5. Matt / wash windows

   **Q:** _____

   **A:** _____

6. Lin and Nancy / walk dogs

   **Q:** _____

   **A:** _____

**1** Look at the underlined information. Then write questions to complete the conversations.

1. **A** *Who's going to serve the pizza?*

   **B** Paulo is going to serve the pizza.

2. **A** _____

   **B** We're going to have the party in the library.

3. **A** _____

   **B** Everyone is going to sign the card.

4. **A** _____

   **B** We're going to eat sandwiches.

5. **A** _____

   **B** Belle is going to wrap the gift.

6. **A** _____

   **B** Alexa is going to pour the drinks.

7. **A** _____

   **B** We're going to have the party at 12:00 p.m.

8. **A** _____

   **B** We're going to set up the snack table over there.

**2** Write questions and answers to complete the conversation.

**Pamela** Hi, Cruz. Let's talk about the farewell party for Mr. Brady.

**Cruz** Great. (when / we / have the party) *When are we going to have the party?*

**Pamela** (next Friday) *We're going to have the party next Friday.* OR *Next Friday.*

**Cruz** OK. (what / we / eat) _____

**Pamela** (pizza and chocolate cake) _____

**Cruz** Mmm. I love chocolate cake.

**Pamela** (where / we / have the party) _____

**Cruz** (the cafeteria) _____

**Pamela** (who / decorate the cafeteria) _____

**Cruz** (Cindy and Mark) _____

**Pamela** Good. (I / give a speech) _____

**Cruz** OK. (who / make the cake) _____

**Pamela** (you) _____

**Cruz** Me? I can't make cakes!

# Mini-review

**1** **Read the article. Then write questions and answers.**

Famous movie stars Mitch Ford and Jessica (Jes) Palmer have exciting plans for the weekend. They're going to go to a fancy party in Los Angeles. Jes and Mitch are going to fly to Los Angeles on Friday night. On Saturday morning, Jes is going to go shopping for a dress to wear to the party. Mitch is going to hang out with his friends. On Saturday afternoon, Jes and Mitch are going to talk to some TV reporters. On Saturday night, Jes and Mitch are going to go to the party. Jes is

going to eat some fancy food, but Mitch isn't. He doesn't like fancy food. After the party, Jes and Mitch are going to fly home.

1. Jes and Mitch / go to a party

    **Q:** *Are Jes and Mitch going to go to a party?*

    **A:** *Yes, they are.*

2. Jes / go shopping

    **Q:** _____

    **A:** _____

3. Mitch / hang out with his brother

    **Q:** _____

    **A:** _____

4. Jes and Mitch / go to the movies

    **Q:** _____

    **A:** _____

5. Mitch / eat some fancy food

    **Q:** _____

    **A:** _____

6. Jes and Mitch / fly home after the party

    **Q:** _____

    **A:** _____

**2** **What are these teens' plans for tomorrow? Look at the chart. Write *Who, What,* or *Where* questions with *be going to.* Then answer the questions.**

| Who | What | Where |
|-----|------|-------|
| Selina | go shopping | at the mall |
| Anthony | walk dogs | in the park |
| Owen | do homework | at the library |

1. **Q:** *What's Selina going to do?*

    **A:** *Selina is going to go shopping.*

2. **Q:** _____

    **A:** _____

3. **Q:** _____

    **A:** _____

4. **Q:** _____

    **A:** _____

5. **Q:** _____

    **A:** _____

6. **Q:** _____

    **A:** _____

## Lesson 23 · Dance clothes

**1** Look at the pictures. Then complete the conversations with *Which one*, *Which ones*, *the one*, or *the ones* and the words in the box.

☐ denim ☐ flowered ☐ plaid ☐ polka-dot ☑ striped ☐ tie-dyed

1. **A** *Which one* is Olivia?
   **B** She's *the one* in the *striped* dress.

2. **A** _____ are Mr. and Mrs. Parker?
   **B** They're _____ in the _____ jackets.

3. **A** _____ is Armando?
   **B** He's _____ in the _____ tie.

4. **A** _____ are the Ramirez brothers?
   **B** They're _____ in the _____ shirts.

5. **A** _____ is Lynn?
   **B** She's _____ in the _____ hat.

6. **A** _____ is Randy?
   **B** He's _____ in the _____ T-shirt.

**2** Write questions and answers.

1. **Q:** (Angelo) *Which one is Angelo?*
   **A:** (polka-dot socks) *He's the one in the polka-dot socks.*

2. **Q:** (José) _____
   **A:** (solid jacket) _____

3. **Q:** (Lois and Isabelle) _____
   **A:** (plaid skirts) _____

4. **Q:** (Rosalie) _____
   **A:** (flowered pants) _____

5. **Q:** (Mr. and Mrs. Clayson) _____
   **A:** (checked shirts) _____

# After the dance

**1** **Look at the picture. Then write questions. Match the questions to the answers.**

1. denim jacket

   **Q:** _Whose denim jacket is this?_ _____f_____        a. They're Juan's.

2. sneakers

   **Q:** _____ _____        b. It's Mel's.

3. hat

   **Q:** _____ _____        c. They're Candy's.

4. comic books

   **Q:** _____ _____        d. It's Delilah's.

5. skateboard

   **Q:** _____ _____        e. They're Leo's.

6. books

   **Q:** _____ _____        f. It's Viv's.

**2** **Look at the pictures. Then write questions and answers. Use possessive pronouns.**

1. **Q:** (camera) _Whose_
   _camera is this?_
   **A:** _It's ours._

2. **Q:** (sunglasses) _____
   _____
   **A:** _____

3. **Q:** (cell phone) _____
   _____
   **A:** _____

4. **Q:** (cat) _____
   _____
   **A:** _____

5. **Q:** (backpack) _____
   _____
   **A:** _____

6. **Q:** (wallet) _____
   _____
   **A:** _____

**1** Read the messages on the Web site quickly. What's Juanita's local library going to do?

_____

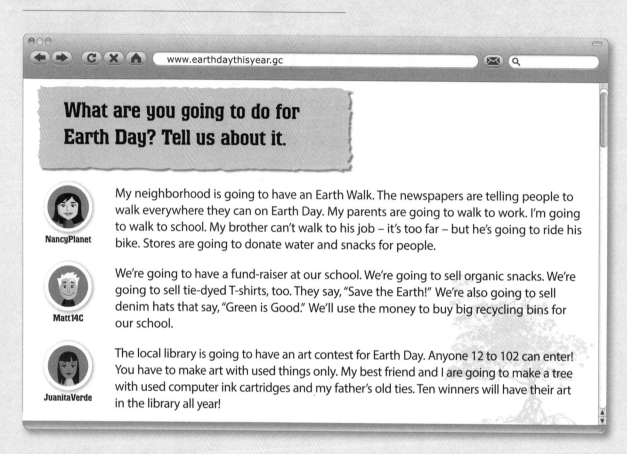

**What are you going to do for Earth Day? Tell us about it.**

**NancyPlanet**

My neighborhood is going to have an Earth Walk. The newspapers are telling people to walk everywhere they can on Earth Day. My parents are going to walk to work. I'm going to walk to school. My brother can't walk to his job – it's too far – but he's going to ride his bike. Stores are going to donate water and snacks for people.

**Matt14C**

We're going to have a fund-raiser at our school. We're going to sell organic snacks. We're going to sell tie-dyed T-shirts, too. They say, "Save the Earth!" We're also going to sell denim hats that say, "Green is Good." We'll use the money to buy big recycling bins for our school.

**JuanitaVerde**

The local library is going to have an art contest for Earth Day. Anyone 12 to 102 can enter! You have to make art with used things only. My best friend and I are going to make a tree with used computer ink cartridges and my father's old ties. Ten winners will have their art in the library all year!

**2** Match the words to the definitions.

1. cartridge _d_
2. used _____
3. fund-raiser _____
4. organic _____
5. donate _____

a. give for free
b. natural
c. an event to get money
d. a case that holds something
e. not new

**3** Read the messages in Part 1 slowly. Answer the questions.

1. Who's going to walk to school? _Nancy is going to walk to school._ OR _Nancy is._ OR _Nancy._

2. How's Nancy's brother going to get to work? _____

3. Whose school is going to sell clothing? _____

4. Who's going to enter the art contest? _____

5. What's the tree going to be made with? _____

**1** Look at the party invitation. Then write questions and answers. Look at the underlined information for help.

**To all students:**

Please come to a farewell party for Mr. Connor.

**When:** Friday, November 7

**Where:** The school library

Pizza, soda, and chocolate cake for everyone! Please sign Mr. Connor's card before the party.

Stay for Mrs. Barber's speech and a special dance by the Spanish club. The teachers are going to give Mr. Connor a farewell gift.

**Everyone:** Please stay after the party to help clean up.

1. **Q:** Where are the students going to have the party?
   **A:** *They're going to have the party in the school library.* OR *In the school library.*

2. **Q:** _____
   **A:** Mrs. Barber is going to <u>give a specch</u>.

3. **Q:** _____
   **A:** The Spanish club is going to <u>perform a special dance</u>.

4. **Q:** _____
   **A:** <u>The teachers</u> are going to give Mr. Connor a farewell gift.

5. **Q:** _____
   **A:** <u>Everyone</u> is going to stay after the party to help clean up.

6. **Q:** What are the students going to eat?
   **A:** _____

7. **Q:** Are the students going to drink tea?
   **A:** _____

8. **Q:** What are the students going to do before the party?
   **A:** _____

**2** Look at the picture. Then complete the conversations. For numbers 3–5, use the correct possessive pronouns.

 **Rick**  **Paola**  **Ty**  **Aiko and Aki**  **Me**

1. **A** (sunglasses) *Whose sunglasses are these?*
   **B** They're Rick's.
   **A** Which one is Rick?
   **B** *He's the one in the checked shirt.*

2. **A** (necklace) _____
   **B** It's Paola's.
   **A** Which one is Paola?
   **B** _____

3. **A** (sneakers) _____
   **B** They're _____ *his* _____ .
   **A** Which one is he?
   **B** _____

4. **A** (hats) _____
   **B** They're _____ .

5. **A** (jacket) _____
   **B** It's _____ .

**1** Complete the sentences with the affirmative or negative past continuous forms of the verbs in the box.

☐ babysit ☐ (not) do ☑ listen to ☐ make dinner ☐ play ☐ (not) read ☐ talk ☐ watch

1. Cecilia *was listening to* an MP3 player in her room.
2. Drew _____ his homework.
   He _____ video games.
3. They _____ an exciting tennis match.
4. Sheila _____ a book.
   She _____ on her cell phone.
5. He _____ his little brother.
6. Mrs. Walker _____ in the kitchen.

**2** What were the people in the pictures doing yesterday? Write past continuous sentences. Use the negative forms of the verbs when necessary.

1. (Tim and Jim / watch TV at home) *Tim and Jim weren't watching TV at home. They were riding a roller coaster.*

2. (Rita / shop at the mall) _____

3. (Manik / do yard work) _____

4. (Jin and Lynn / walk dogs) _____

5. (you / ride your bike in the park) _____

6. (Kendra / take pictures with her new camera) _____

**UNIT 7 Our Stories**

44

# Scary experiences

**1 Choose the correct forms of the verbs to complete the sentences.**

1. Tara _____fell_____ (was falling / fell) when she
   _was skateboarding___ (was skateboarding / skateboarded).

2. We _____ (ate / were eating) lunch when the fire
   alarm _____ (was ringing / rang).

3. I _____ (was listening / listened) to music when
   I _____ (fell / was falling) asleep!

4. They _____ (watched / were watching) TV when
   a man _____ (was knocking / knocked) on the door.

5. Mrs. Montoya _____ (was making / made) lunch
   when the baby _____ (started / was starting) to cry.

6. The man _____ (was shouting / shouted) when we
   _____ (arrived / were arriving) at the zoo.

**2 Look at the chart. Then write sentences with *when*. Use the correct
forms of the verbs or verb phrases in the chart.**

| Name | Action in progress | Action completed |
|------|--------------------|--------------------|
| 1. Carlos and Trina | drive to work | see a cat in the street |
| 2. Beth | sleep | someone knock at the door |
| 3. Diego | watch TV | the phone ring |
| 4. Anna and Mariano | make dinner | the electricity go out |
| 5. Tom | play soccer | fall and hurt his leg |

1. _Carlos and Trina were driving to work when they saw a cat in the street._

2. _____

3. _____

4. _____

5. _____

**3 Complete the statements with the simple past or the past continuous.
Use your own information.**

1. I was _____ when the alarm clock
   rang this morning.

2. When I got home yesterday, _____ .

3. When I arrived at school this morning, _____
   _____ .

4. I was _____ when the phone rang
   yesterday.

# Mini-review

**1 Rewrite the sentences in the past continuous.**

1. Ellen asks the singer for an autograph. _Ellen was asking the singer for an autograph._

2. The dog barks at the bird in the tree. _____

3. Eduardo surfs the Internet for information. _____

4. Mr. Lauer drives his kids to soccer practice. _____

5. Nicole and Lena talk on the phone. _____

6. Roy takes pictures of his family. _____

**2 Look at the pictures. Then complete the sentences with _when_ and the correct forms of the verb phrases in the box.**

- ☐ do his homework / hear a noise
- ☐ wind start to blow / do yard work
- ☐ eat dinner / phone ring
- ☑ in-line skate / start to rain
- ☐ electricity go out / play a video game
- ☐ watch TV / fall asleep

1. Wendy _was in-line skating when it started to rain_ .

2. Beto _____

_____ .

3. Mr. and Mrs. Thomas

_____ .

4. Abi _____

_____ .

5. _____ ,

we _____ .

6. _____ ,

Doug _____ .

**1** **Write questions to complete the conversations.**

1. (they / skateboard) **Q:** _Were they skateboarding?_ **A:** Yes, they were.

2. (you / walk) **Q:** _____ **A:** We were walking in the park.

3. (it / rain) **Q:** _____ **A:** Yes, it was.

4. (you / do) **Q:** _____ **A:** We were white-water rafting.

5. (they / surf) **Q:** _____ **A:** No, they weren't.

6. (you / play) **Q:** _____ **A:** We were playing basketball.

7. (Sheila / study) **Q:** _____ **A:** She was studying in the library.

8. (the sun / shine) **Q:** _____ **A:** No, it wasn't.

**2** **Read the story. Then complete the questions with the past continuous. Answer the questions.**

A year ago, Marty Long and his one-year-old cousin were playing together in the backyard. Marty's small dog, Zoey, was with them. It was a nice, hot summer day and they were all having a good time.

While they were playing, Zoey suddenly started running toward Marty's cousin and barking loudly. Marty ran to them and saw Zoey between the little boy and a big rattlesnake! Zoey was trying to stop the rattlesnake from biting Marty's cousin. Sadly, the snake bit Zoey on the head. Marty quickly took her to a nearby animal hospital, and a few days later she was fine. Zoey's story is now on a Web site for pet heroes.

1. **Q:** What _were_ Marty and his cousin _doing_ in the backyard? (do)

   **A:** _They were playing._ _____

2. **Q:** Who _____ with them? (play)

   **A:** _____

3. **Q:** _____ it _____? (rain)

   **A:** _____

4. **Q:** What happened while they _____? (play)

   **A:** _____

5. **Q:** What _____ Zoey _____ at? (bark)

   **A:** _____

6. **Q:** What _____ Zoey _____ to do? (try)

   **A:** _____

# Sharing stories

**1** **Underline the simple past verb in each sentence. Then circle the past continuous verb in each sentence.**

1. My dog <u>saw</u> a squirrel while he (was running) in the woods.
2. Mrs. Letterman's cell phone rang while she was driving her car.
3. While we were practicing soccer, I hurt my wrist.
4. Hugo ate his dinner while his mother was washing the dishes.
5. We made our campfire while the sun was shining.
6. Jody and Tom got lost while they were riding their bikes in the park.
7. We told scary stories while we were sitting around the campfire.
8. While Allison was chatting online, her brother made dinner.

**2** **Write the simple past and past continuous forms of each verb.**

1. fly _____flew_____ _____was flying_____    7. run _____ _____
2. hear _____ _____    8. read _____ _____
3. move _____ _____    9. write _____ _____
4. start _____ _____    10. sleep _____ _____
5. eat _____ _____    11. call _____ _____
6. touch _____ _____    12. laugh _____ _____

**3** **Complete the story with the simple past or the past continuous forms of the verbs in the box.**

| ☐ do | ☐ hear | ☐ laugh | ☐ make | ☐ run | ☐ turn on |
| ☐ feel | ☐ help | ☐ look | ☐ (not) see | ☐ scream | ☑ watch |

Anita _was watching_ TV in the living room. It was dark. She
_____ a strange noise. Anita _____ around the
living room. She _____ anything unusual. Her mother
_____ dinner in the kitchen. Her father _____
her mother make dinner. Her brothers _____ homework
upstairs. She heard the noise again. This time it was louder. All
of a sudden, Anita _____ something on her back.
Anita _____! Anita's mother and father _____
into the living room and _____ the light. "What's wrong?"
they yelled. Anita turned around and saw her cat, Purrfect.
Anita _____ and said she was sorry. Her parents
laughed, too.

**1** **Read the article quickly. What number did Chuck call?**

## An Unusual Rescuc

We have a new hero right here in Marvindale. Last week, Chuck Edgers was watching the news when he heard a cat meowing loudly. The sound was coming from his neighbor's house. He went to the house, knocked on the front door, but no one answered. The meow got louder. He went to the back of the house. The back door was unlocked, so he pushed it open.

His neighbor, Fred Williams, was sleeping on the couch when Chuck entered the living room. He shook Mr. Williams but he would not wake up. Chuck carried Mr. Williams outside and called 911.

The rescue workers came and helped Mr. Williams. They went into the house and later said his carbon monoxide alarm wasn't working. The cat and Mr. Edgers saved Mr. Williams!

**2** **Check (✓) the correct answers.**

1. **A** I read a great book about Nelson Mandela.

   **B** ☐ Really? He rescued my cat.     ☑ Really? He's my hero.

2. **A** What's something you need in your house to keep you safe?

   **B** ☐ A carbon monoxide alarm.     ☐ A cat.

3. **A** My cat was on the roof when I got home from school. It couldn't get down.

   **B** ☐ Who rescued it?     ☐ Does it meow?

4. **A** How do you open this door?

   **B** ☐ You enter.     ☐ You push it open.

**3** **Read the article in Part 1 slowly. Complete the sentences with *before*, *after*, or *when*.**

1. Mr. Edgers was watching the news _____*when*_____ he heard a cat meowing.

2. Mr. Edgers went to the front door _____ he went to the back door.

3. Mr. Williams was sleeping _____ Chuck entered his house.

4. Chuck called 911 _____ he was outside.

5. A rescue worker came to the house _____ Chuck called 911.

**1  Match the questions to the answers.**

1. Was it windy? _f_

2. What was Sylvia doing? ____

3. Were Mr. and Mrs. Smith watching TV? ____

4. Where was Dan last night? ____

5. What were Brett and Helena doing? ____

6. Was Miranda skiing last weekend? ____

a. He was at the library.

b. They were playing video games.

c. She was buying a new DVD player.

d. Yes, she was.

e. No, they weren't.

f. Yes, it was.

**2  Complete the conversation with the sentences in the box.**

☐ It was raining very hard.  ☐ Well, I was walking along Stewart Street when I saw something weird.
☐ I was going to the store.  ☑ What were you doing?
☐ No, she wasn't.  ☐ Where were you going?
☐ Was your sister with you?  ☐ You saw a bear when you were walking to the store?

**Henry**  Hey, Ben. I heard you had a scary experience last night. _What were you doing?_

**Ben**  _____

**Henry**  Wow. What did you see?

**Ben**  I'm not sure. _____

**Henry**  That's right. It was very rainy last night. _____

**Ben**  _____ She had a cold, so she stayed home.

**Henry**  _____ Were you going home?

**Ben**  No, I wasn't. _____ I wanted some ice cream. You're going to think I'm crazy, but I think I saw a bear.

**Henry**  _____ You're right! I do think you're crazy!

**3  Complete the sentences with both the simple past and the past continuous.**

1. do homework

   I _did my homework_____ .

   I _was doing my homework_____ .

2. not cry

   The baby _____ .

   The baby _____ .

3. shop at the music store

   You _____ .

   You _____ .

4. not watch the movie

   Joan and Alan _____ .

   Joan and Alan _____ .

5. not snow

   It _____ .

   It _____ .

6. use the Internet

   Nicholas _____ .

   Nicholas _____ .

# How do I get there?

**1 Complete the conversation with the words in the box.**

☐ across ☑ go past ☐ on the corner ☐ turn left
☐ cross ☐ go straight ☐ on your right

**Candy** Stan, how do I get to
your apartment? I'm in front
of the subway entrance.

**Stan** Oh, that's easy. Turn left and
_go past_ the bank.

**Candy** OK.

**Stan** At the second intersection,
_____ the street.
Then _____ . There's
a nail salon _____ .

**Candy** Uh-huh. And then?

**Stan** Then _____ ahead
on K Street.

**Candy** OK. Is your apartment
building _____ ?

**Stan** Yes, it's on the corner. The
entrance is _____
from the flower shop.

clothing store, post office, grocery store, laundromat, Main Road, subway entrance, nail salon, K Street, M Street, bank, newsstand, bakery, video store, restaurant, Grand Street, Stan's apartment, flower shop, health club, skyscraper

**2 Look at the map in Part 1. Then correct the statements.**

1. The newsstand is between the bakery and the health club.

   _The newsstand is on the corner, next to the bakery._

2. The video store is on the corner, across from the restaurant.

   _____

3. (You're at the grocery store.) Turn right and go straight. Go past the post office.
   Cross the next intersection. The clothing store is on your left.

   _____

4. (You're at the flower shop.) Turn right and go straight on K Street to the second
   intersection. Turn left onto Main Road to get to the post office.

   _____

5. (You're at the restaurant.) Turn right and go past the video store, newsstand,
   and bakery. Turn right onto K Street. Go straight ahead. The nail salon is on
   the right, on the next corner.

   _____

**1** Alejandro is writing an article for the school newspaper about a street fair. Look at his list of things that were (✔) and weren't (✗) at the street fair. Write sentences with *There was a / some*, *There were some*, *There wasn't any*, and *There weren't any*.

Pine Street Fair

✔ good food 🍔　✔ rides

✗ ice cream 🍦　✔ games

✔ a hot-dog stand　✗ a raffle

✔ a ticket booth　✗ street vendors

1. *There was some good food.*

2. _____

3. _____

4. _____

5. _____

6. _____

7. _____

8. _____

**2** Write questions with *Was there* and *Were there*. Then write answers.

1. **Q:** (any books for sale) *Were there any books for sale?*

   **A:** (yes) *Yes, there were.*

2. **Q:** (a pizza stand) _____

   **A:** (no) _____

3. **Q:** (music) _____

   **A:** (yes) _____

4. **Q:** (flowers for sale) _____

   **A:** (no) _____

**3** Think about a party you attended. Write sentences with positive and negative forms of *There was a* and *There were some*. Use the words in the box and your own information.

☐ cake　☑ games　☐ ice cream　☐ pizza
☐ dancing　☐ gifts　☐ music　☐ snacks

1. *There weren't any games.*

2. _____

3. _____

4. _____

5. _____

6. _____

7. _____

8. _____

# Mini-review

**1** Look at the map. Livvie is new in town. She is in front of her apartment building on Kelly Street. Write answers to her questions.

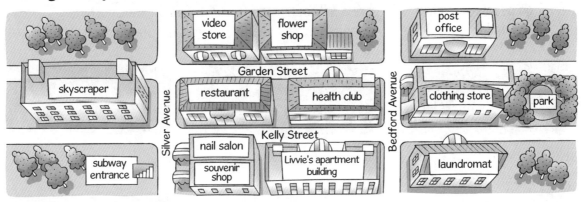

1. **Q:** How do I get to the health club?

   **A:** *Go to the corner of Bedford Avenue and Kelly Street. Turn left at the intersection.*

      *Go straight ahead. Turn left onto Garden Street. The health club is on the left.*

2. **Q:** How do I get to the post office?

   **A:** _____

   _____

3. **Q:** How do I get to the park?

   **A:** _____

   _____

4. **Q:** How do I get to the video store?

   **A:** _____

   _____

**2** Trina tells Luis about her vacation. Complete the conversation with *was there, were there, there was, there were,* and the cues.

Luis  Hi, Trina. How was your vacation?

Trina  Hi, Luis. It was fantastic. I went on a cruise to Mexico.

Luis  (any kids your age) *Were there any kids your age?*

Trina  (yes) _____ I made some new friends.

Luis  (any activities on the cruise) _____

Trina  (yes) _____ (a few teen parties) _____

Luis  Wow! That sounds great. (a lot of good food) _____

Trina  (yes) _____ I ate delicious food every day!

Luis  Did you go shopping on the cruise?

Trina  No, I didn't. _____ a few stores, but everything was too expensive.

# Things to do

**1** Look at the pictures. Then write suggestions with the words in the box.

☐ go people-watching    ☐ take a helicopter ride    ☑ try public transportation
☐ go window-shopping    ☐ try an ethnic restaurant    ☐ visit the Statue of Liberty

1. _We could try public transportation._

2. _____

3. _____

4. _____

5. _____

6. _____

**2** Write suggestions for 1–4. Write preferences for a–d. Then match the suggestions to the preferences.

1. try an ethnic restaurant

   **A** _We could try an ethnic restaurant._ OR

     _Why don't we try an ethnic restaurant?_   _c_

     a. go to a concert

     **B** _____

2. take a taxi

   **A** _____

     b. visit a famous landmark

     **B** _____

3. visit a museum

   **A** _____

     c. eat a hamburger

     **B** _I'd rather eat a hamburger._

4. go to a movie

   **A** _____

     d. take the bus

     **B** _____

**3** Which would you rather do? Write sentences about your preferences.

1. go skateboarding / go biking _I'd rather go skateboarding._

2. sleep late / go to bed early _____

3. clean my room / do homework _____

4. go to a party / go to a movie _____

5. take a boat ride / take a helicopter ride _____

6. eat pizza / try an ethnic restaurant _____

# We didn't go...

**1** **Rewrite the sentences with the simple past and *because*.**

1. Eva goes to Little Italy. She wants Italian food.

   *Eva went to Little Italy because she wanted Italian food.*

2. Grace doesn't walk to the hotel. She catches the bus.

   _____

3. Will and Carolina don't call their parents. They forget.

   _____

4. Eliza eats in a fast-food restaurant. She wants a hamburger.

   _____

5. Antonio goes to the museum. He wants to see the nature exhibit.

   _____

6. Patricia stays home from school. She isn't feeling well.

   _____

**2** **Look at the list of things Kelly and Matt did (✓) and didn't (X) do on their family vacation to Colorado. Then write sentences with *because*.**

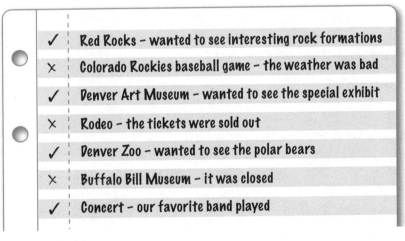

| | |
|---|---|
| ✓ | Red Rocks – wanted to see interesting rock formations |
| X | Colorado Rockies baseball game – the weather was bad |
| ✓ | Denver Art Museum – wanted to see the special exhibit |
| X | Rodeo – the tickets were sold out |
| ✓ | Denver Zoo – wanted to see the polar bears |
| X | Buffalo Bill Museum – it was closed |
| ✓ | Concert – our favorite band played |

1. (visit Red Rocks) *We visited Red Rocks because we wanted to see interesting rock formations.*

2. (go to baseball game) _____

3. (visit art museum) _____

4. (go to rodeo) _____

5. (go to zoo) _____

6. (visit museum) _____

7. (go to concert) _____

**1** Read the Web site quickly. Check (✓) the things you can do in Oahu.

☐ go on the subway    ☐ visit a beach    ☐ visit a harbor

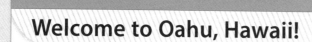

www.touristinformationoffice.gc

## Welcome to Oahu, Hawaii!

There are many things to do here!

Visit Waikiki Beach. Enjoy the sunshine and swim in Oahu's

warm water. It's also a great place to go shopping.

Go to a luau. Eat traditional Hawaiian food and watch traditional Hawaiian dances.

Visit Pearl Harbor. It's a national historic site. See the USS Missouri. It's not a cruise ship. It was a war ship and now it's a museum.

Take a helicopter ride. See Oahu's beaches and rain forest from the sky.

The tourist information office has all the information you need. Visit us every day from 9:00 a.m. – 6:00 p.m.

**2** Complete the sentences with the underlined words in Part 1.

1. **A** Why don't we fly to Puerto Rico?
   **B** I'd rather take a _cruise ship_ .

2. **A** Let's go window-shopping downtown.
   **B** I'd rather _____ in the plaza.

3. **A** Is the Alamo in Texas a famous fort?
   **B** Yes. In fact, it's a _____ .

4. We took a _____ because we wanted to have a good view of the harbor.

5. We went to the _____ because the information wasn't online.

**3** Read the Web site in Part 1 slowly. Circle the correct words to complete the sentences.

1. This is the (museum's / ⓣourist information office's) Web site.
2. You can (take a helicopter ride / go shopping) at Waikiki Beach.
3. You can try Hawaiian food at a (historic site / luau).
4. Go to (Pearl Harbor / Waikiki Beach) to visit a museum.
5. See the rain forest from (the beach / a helicopter).

**1** Look at the map. Complete the questions with *Was there* and *Were there*. Then answer the questions. Complete the directions with the words in the box.

Rudy's Restaurant

Apple Street

Main Street

Cool Clothing Store

Apple Street

The Little Café

health club

bookstore

post office

☐ across the street   ☐ cross   ☐ go past   ☑ on the corner   ☐ turn left

**A** I went to a great little town last weekend.

**B** Really? What was it like? *Was there* a clothing store?

**A** *Yes, there was.* It was *on the corner* of Main and Apple Streets.

**B** _____ any good restaurants?

**A** _____ Rudy's Restaurant was on Apple Street, and The Little Café was _____ from Rudy's.

**B** _____ a flower shop?

**A** _____

**B** _____ a health club?

**A** _____ It was on Main Street.

**B** If I go to this little town, how do I get to the health club?

**A** Well, if you're at the post office on Apple Street, _____ the bookstore. _____ the intersection. _____ onto Main Street. It's on your right.

**2** Rewrite the sentences as suggestions, preferences, or sentences with *because*.

1. I wanted to see the mystery movie. (suggestion) *Why don't we see the mystery movie?*
   My friend wanted to see the romance movie.
   (preference) *She'd rather see the romance movie.*
   We went to the mystery movie. The tickets for the romance movie were sold out!
   (sentence with *because*) *We went to the mystery movie because the tickets for the romance movie were sold out.*

2. My friend and I wanted to eat at a restaurant.
   I wanted to try Indian food. (suggestion) _____
   My friend wanted to try Japanese food. (preference) _____
   We didn't eat Japanese food. The Japanese restaurant was closed!
   (sentence with *because*) _____

## Illustration Credits

**Adolar** 6, 24, 41, 51, 53, 57

**Chuck Gonzales** 8, 12, 18, 31, 39, 44

**Marcelo Pacheco** 15, 37, 46

**Paulo Borges** 4, 29, 38, 43, 48

**Terry Wong** 3, 27, 30, 40, 42

**Pamela Hobbs** 17

## Photo Acknowledgements

The authors and publishers acknowledge the following sources of copyright material and are grateful for the permissions granted. While every effort has been made, it has not always been possible to identify the sources of all the material used, or to trace all copyright holders. If any omissions are brought to our notice, we will be happy to include the appropriate acknowledgements on reprinting.

### Workbook

p. 3: ©Juniors Bildarchiv GmbH/Alamy; p. 7: ©Horst Herget/Masterfile; p. 9: ©Stockbyte/Getty Images; p. 10: ©jgorzynik/Shutterstock; p. 11 (T): ©Purestock/Getty Images; p. 11 (C): ©Charles Smith/Corbis; p. 11 (B): ©Nancy Ney/CORBIS; p. 13: ©Comstock/Stockbyte/Getty Images; p. 14 (T): ©Images of Africa Photobank/Alamy; p. 14 (C): ©bouzou/Shutterstock; p. 14 (B): ©Alfie Photography/Shutterstock; p. 15: ©Julian Love/AWL Images/Getty Images; p. 16: ©Peter G. Balazsy/age fotostock/Getty Images; p. 19: ©CORBIS; p. 20: ©Time Life Pictures/NASA/The LIFE Picture Collection/Getty Images; p. 21: ©WorldFoto/Alamy; p. 23: ©Cherryson/Shutterstock; p. 25 (L): ©Xinhua/Alamy; p. 25 (C): ©epa european pressphoto agency b.v./Alamy; p. 25 (R): ©Amy Sussman/Getty Images; p. 26 (T): ©Alexander Hassenstein/Getty Images; p. 26 (CL): ©DEA PICTURE LIBRARY/Getty Images; p. 26 (CR): ©Herschel Hoffmeyer/Shutterstock; p. 26 (BL): ©De Agostini Picture Library/De Agostini/Getty Images; p. 26 (BC): ©Andreas Meyer/Shutterstock; p. 26 (BR): ©Universal Images Group Limited/Alamy; p. 27 (T): ©Maremagnum/Photodisc/Getty Images; p. 27 (B): ©vichie81/Shutterstock; p. 28 (TL): ©Oksana Perkins/iStock/Getty Images Plus/Getty Images; p. 28 (TR): ©Art Kowalsky/Alamy; p. 28 (BL): ©Alistair Baird/Alamy; p. 28 (BR): ©Armin Rose/Shutterstock; p. 32 (T): ©Losevsky Pavel/Shutterstock; p. 32 (B): ©Ruslan Guzov/Shutterstock; p. 33: ©MANDY GODBEHEAR/Shutterstock; p. 34: ©rubberball/Getty Images; p. 35 (T): ©Fuse/Getty Images; p. 35 (B): ©Yadid Levy/Robert Harding World Imagery/Getty Images; p. 36: ©Muriel de Seze/Digital Vision/Getty Images; p. 37: ©Fuse/Getty Images; p. 45 (T): ©BananaStock/Getty Images Plus/Getty Images; p. 45 (B): ©Rich Legg/Stock/Getty Images Plus/Getty Images; p. 47 (T): ©RGB Ventures/SuperStock/Alamy; p. 47 (B): ©Rick & Nora Bowers/Alamy; p. 49: ©Georg Bochem/Corbis; p. 54 (TL): ©Kevin Foy/Alamy; p. 54 (TC): ©Image Source/Getty Images; p. 54 (TR): ©Katharina M/Shutterstock; p. 54 (BL): ©Norbert Schaefer/Corbis; p. 54 (BC): ©Mitchell Funk/Photographer's Choice/Getty Images; p. 54 (BR): ©Thinkstock/Stockbyte/Getty Images; p. 55 (T): Picturenet/Blend Images/Getty Images; p. 55 (B): ©Lunnderboy/iStock/Getty Images Plus/Getty Images; p. 56 (L): ©Stock Connection Blue/Alamy; p. 56 (R): ©Ilene MacDonald/Alamy.

**Cover photograph** by ©A. T. Willett/Alamy.

# Notes

# Notes

# Notes

# Notes